SNOW

BILL McAULIFFE

WEATHER X BOOKS

CREATIVE EDUCATION   CREATIVE PAPERBACKS

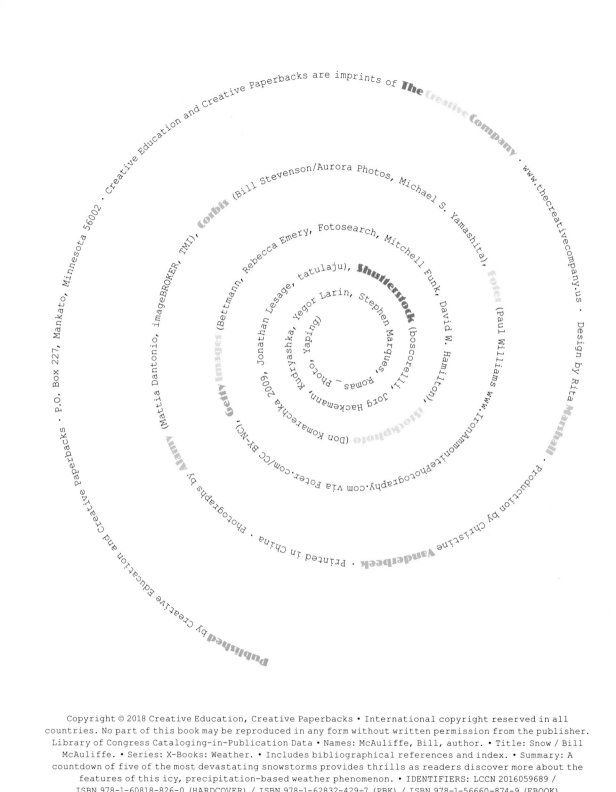
Copyright © 2018 Creative Education, Creative Paperbacks • International copyright reserved in all countries. No part of this book may be reproduced in any form without written permission from the publisher. Library of Congress Cataloging-in-Publication Data • Names: McAuliffe, Bill, author. • Title: Snow / Bill McAuliffe. • Series: X-Books: Weather. • Includes bibliographical references and index. • Summary: A countdown of five of the most devastating snowstorms provides thrills as readers discover more about the features of this icy, precipitation-based weather phenomenon. • IDENTIFIERS: LCCN 2016059689 / ISBN 978-1-60818-826-0 (HARDCOVER) / ISBN 978-1-62832-429-7 (PBK) / ISBN 978-1-56660-874-9 (EBOOK) Subjects: LCSH: Snow–Juvenile literature. • CLASSIFICATION: LCC QC926.37.M42 2017 / DDC 551.57/84–dc23 CCSS: RI.3.1–8; RI.4.1–5, 7; RI.5.1–3, 8; RI.6.1–2, 4, 7; RH.6–8.3–8 First Edition HC 9 8 7 6 5 4 3 2 1 • First Edition PBK 9 8 7 6 5 4 3 2 1

3-28-18

SNOW

CONTENTS

Xtraordinary
WEATHER 5

Xciting
FACTS 28

Xtreme
TOP 5 SNOWSTORMS
#5 10
#4 16
#3 22
#2 26
#1 31

Xtensive
SNOWFALL 24

Xceptional
SNOWFALL 18

Xasperating
SNOW 20

GLOSSARY
RESOURCES
INDEX 32

WEATHER X BOOKS

SNOWFLAKES six-sided clusters of ice crystals

XTRAORDINARY WEATHER

Snow is ice. It forms in cold weather and falls from clouds. Many people enjoy snow. It can be beautiful. But it can also be dangerous.

Snow Basics

People who live in cold places know how to drive in snow. They know how to dress for it and how to get rid of it. Around the world, people have learned to have fun in the snow. They ski and sled. They toss snowballs. They make snow angels and build snowmen. Some people travel to places where there is a lot of snow. They celebrate it with carnivals. They host winter sports events. These people love snow. But they also know to fear it.

The National Oceanic and Atmospheric Administration (NOAA) has more than 120 weather stations across the United States. Snowfall at these stations is measured in inches.

Washington
65

Montana
48

Oregon
47

Idaho
31

Wyoming
49

Nevada
36

California
67

Utah
38

Colorado
75.8

Alaska
78

Arizona
38

New Mexico
41

Hawaii
6.5

GREATEST SNOW DEPTH:

451 inches (1,146 cm), March 1911

Tamarack, California

GREATEST SNOWFALL IN ONE STORM:

189 inches (480 cm), February 1959

Mount Shasta, California

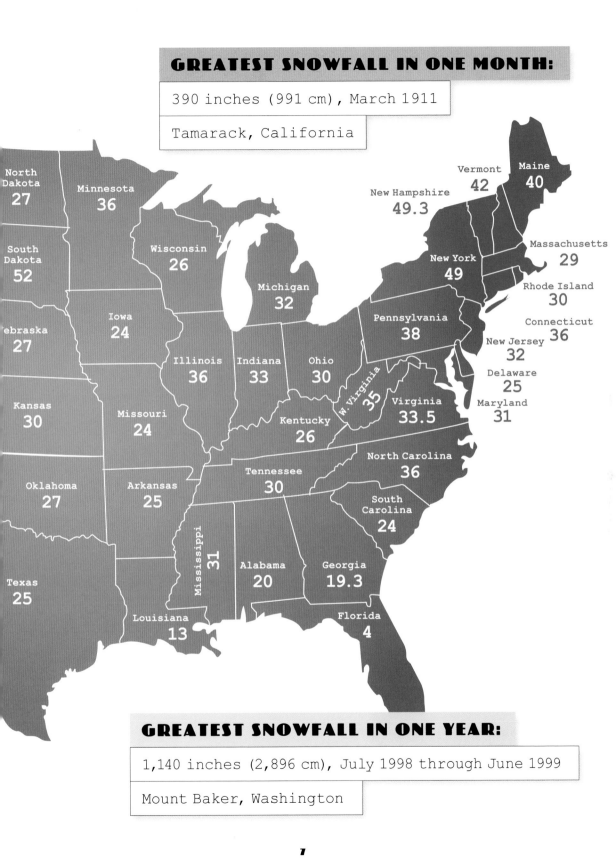

GREATEST SNOWFALL IN ONE MONTH:

390 inches (991 cm), March 1911

Tamarack, California

North Dakota 27

Minnesota 36

Vermont 42

Maine 40

New Hampshire 49.3

South Dakota 52

Wisconsin 26

New York 49

Massachusetts 29

Michigan 32

Rhode Island 30

Nebraska 27

Iowa 24

Pennsylvania 38

Connecticut 36

New Jersey 32

Delaware 25

Kansas 30

Missouri 24

Illinois 36

Indiana 33

Ohio 30

W. Virginia 35

Virginia 33.5

Maryland 31

Kentucky 26

North Carolina 36

Oklahoma 27

Arkansas 25

Tennessee 30

South Carolina 24

Texas 25

Mississippi 31

Alabama 20

Georgia 19.3

Louisiana 13

Florida 4

GREATEST SNOWFALL IN ONE YEAR:

1,140 inches (2,896 cm), July 1998 through June 1999

Mount Baker, Washington

A snowflake is made up of ice crystals.

All ice crystals have six sides.

Ice crystals freeze together.

They form six-sided snowflakes.

SIX-SIDED SNOWFLAKES

Snow can cause many problems. It can slide down a mountainside in an avalanche. An avalanche will bury anything—and anyone—in its path. **Blizzards** are dangerous winter storms. When snowfall is heavy, it can make roofs collapse. It can break power lines, too. Sometimes it even cuts off heat to buildings. Snow often closes roads, airports, and schools. It can shut down entire towns for days.

No two snowflakes are identical.

SNOWFLAKE SHAPES

Snowflakes that fall together may look similar.

Snowflakes can be sorted into groups based on shape.

Xtreme Snowstorm #5

The Donner Party was a group of 87 pioneers. They were traveling to California in 1846. They did not reach the Sierra Nevada Mountains until late October. The trails were already covered in snow. By November, the group was trapped. Snow stood 12 feet (3.7 m) deep. Many of them starved to death. Some resorted to **cannibalism**. Only 41 of the party survived the winter.

Avalanches kill more than 150 people
around the world each year.

NOVEMBER 1846–APRIL 1847

Snow Formation

Snow needs cold air to form. If it forms in temperatures near 32 °F (0 °C), it will be wet and heavy. This is usually good packing snow. Snow that forms in colder temperatures is often light and fluffy.

As the sun warms the ground, water **evaporates**. Water vapor is carried upward with rising warm air. High above the ground, it meets cooler air. This makes it condense, or turn into tiny water droplets. The droplets gather to form a cloud. Inside the cloud, the droplets freeze into ice crystals. Ice crystals then freeze together. This forms a snowflake. When it becomes heavy enough, the snow falls from the cloud.

Falling snowflakes meet many forces. Winds blow the flakes up and down. They may melt and refreeze. Snowflakes hit each other as they fall. They may hit dust and pollutants, too. Such forces reshape snowflakes as they fall to the ground.

plates

hollow columns

25 to 32 °F (−4 to 0 °C)	21 to 25 °F (−6 to −4 °C)	14 to 21 °F (−10 to −6 °C)

needles

branching stars

hollow columns

10 to 14 °F	3 to 10 °F	-8 to 3 °F	below -8 °F
(-12 to -10 °C)	(-16 to -12 °C)	(-22 to -16 °C)	(below -22 °C)

plates

plates

SNOW FORMATION FACT

Water can freeze around snowflakes as they fall.

This forms small, cloudy ice pellets known as graupel.

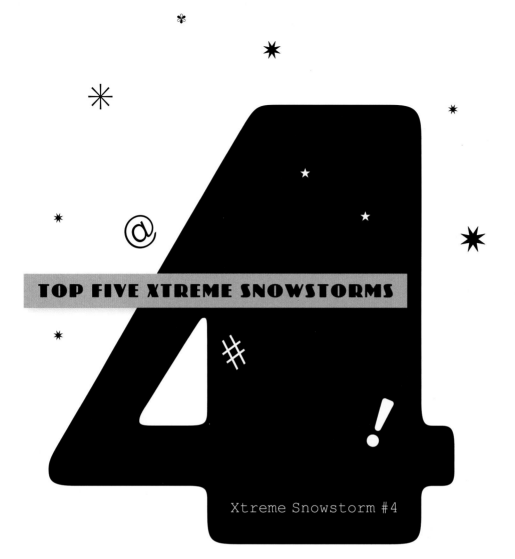

TOP FIVE XTREME SNOWSTORMS

Xtreme Snowstorm #4

The Chicago Blizzard of '79 dumped nearly 20 inches (50.8 cm) of snow on Chicago. The storm killed 99 people. Roofs collapsed. Garbage trucks couldn't pick up trash. Commuter trains failed. At the time, O'Hare was the world's busiest airport. Only half of its runways were open six days after the storm. Chicago blamed the mayor, Michael Bilandic, for poor management. Six weeks later, he lost the mayoral race.

JANUARY 13–14, 1979

XCEPTIONAL SNOWFALL

Many people associate cold with snow. But cold places are not necessarily snowy. Snow is most likely to form between 15 and 32 °F (−9 and 0 °C).

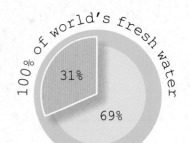

100% of world's fresh water

31%

69%

ice caps and glaciers

bodies of water

SNOWFALL OCCURRENCES FACT

The only time snow fell in Miami, Florida, was on January 19, 1977.

It was not a measurable snowfall. It melted quickly.

Antarctica is a desert. Very little snow falls there.

THE SOUTH POLE

Snowfall Occurrences

Air below 0 °F (-18 °C) has much less water vapor than air that is just below freezing. Water vapor and cold air are necessary for snow to form. Snow usually falls in the far Northern or Southern hemispheres. But it also falls on high mountains elsewhere. Mount Cayambe is near the **equator** in Ecuador. Because it is so tall, its peak is capped with snow year round.

The snowiest major city in the world is Aomori, Japan. Nearly 300,000 people live there. The city is near mountains. It gets 312 inches (792 cm) of snow each year.

Snow has fallen in every state in the U.S. Every year, snow falls on Hawaii's three highest volcanoes. Valdez, Alaska, tops the list of snowy U.S. cities. It averages 326 inches (828 cm) every year. Marquette, Michigan, is the snowiest U.S. city east of the Rocky Mountains. It gets about 204 inches (518 cm) of snow each winter.

XASPERATING SNOW

Snow is a valuable resource. Much of the water used by people today comes from melted snow. But too much snow can be a bad thing.

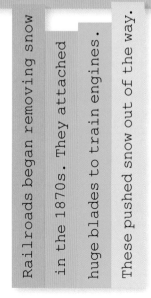

Railroads began removing snow in the 1870s. They attached huge blades to train engines. These pushed snow out of the way.

Almost 75 percent of the water used in the western U.S. comes from snow in the Rocky Mountains. That snow waters crops in the Midwest, too. Snow also protects plants in winter. Roots are less likely to freeze beneath snow-covered ground.

Winter snow can bring danger. In January 1888, a blizzard hit the Midwest. The temperature dropped 18 degrees in 3 minutes. Hundreds of people died. Many were children. They were trapped in schoolhouses. Or they got lost in the storm as they tried to get home. Today, that event is known as the Children's Blizzard.

Snow warnings have improved with time. But snow removal remains a huge—and expensive—task. Even as plows, salt, and other machines move snow, it continues to interrupt daily life. When snow falls fast and heavy, power outages can occur. Traffic slows to a crawl. Vehicles may get stuck or slide off the road.

Xtreme Snowstorm #3

The Storm of the Century hit the U.S. in March 1993. Its deep snow and high winds hit 26 states. No other winter storm has affected such a wide area. It left more than 12 inches (30.5 cm) of snow in Birmingham, Alabama. Snow is rare there. Forty inches (102 cm) fell in Syracuse, New York. About 270 people in the U.S. died. The storm was as strong as a Category 3 hurricane.

MARCH 12–14, 1993

Snowfall can range
from a light dusting
to feet at a time.
Measuring it isn't as
easy as people think.

Measuring Snowfall

Snow is measured on a wooden board. The board is
painted a light color. Each side should be between 16
and 24 inches (40.6–61 cm) long. The board is placed
away from buildings or trees. It should be in a spot
where it will not be bothered. When snowfall ends, a
ruler is stuck straight into the snow.

Seems easy, right? It isn't that simple. Wind can
blow snow into deep drifts. Meanwhile, it can clear the
ground in other spots. Sunlight can melt snow before it
is measured. And wet snow packs down.

To help get a true total, several measurements
are taken. They can be on the board or in a small,
undisturbed area. The average of those numbers is given
as the total snowfall. Then the board is wiped off.

Measurements can be taken during a snowfall, too.

The board should be cleared no more than four times per day.

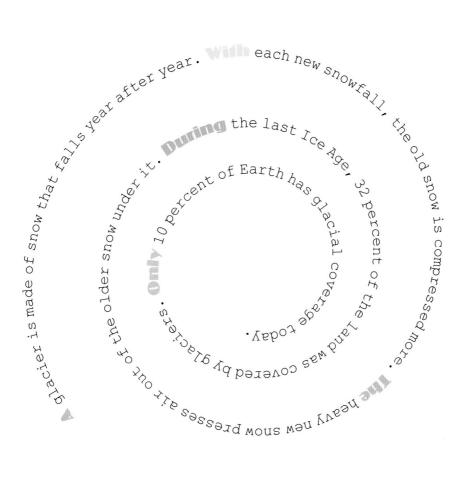

A glacier is made of snow that falls year after year. With each new snowfall, the old snow is compressed more. The heavy new snow presses air out of the older snow under it. During the last Ice Age, 32 percent of the land was covered by glaciers. Only 10 percent of Earth has glacial coverage today.

MEASURING SNOWFALL FACT

During a January 2016 snowstorm, the official weather station in Washington, D.C., lost its board in the snow.

Xtreme Snowstorm #2

The Great Blizzard of 1888 On March 11, 1888, temperatures in the northeastern U.S. dropped. Rain turned to snow. Late that night, a storm hit. It dropped more than 50 inches (127 cm) of snow in some places. High winds formed deep drifts. Ships at sea were wrecked. About 200 people died in New York City alone. Across the region, more than 400 people died. It was the deadliest winter storm in U.S. history.

MARCH 11–12, 1888

As many as 200 ice crystals can make up a snowflake.

Skiing became part of the Olympics in 1924.

Skiing and snowshoeing emerged between 6,000 and 8,000 years ago.

The Russians developed the first snowmobile in the early 20th century.

Snowfall in most of the U.S. has been declining since 1930.

Snow melting high in the mountains often causes spring floods.

When it's very cold, snow will squeak when stepped on.
It's the sound of ice crystals crunching.

For hundreds of years, people in the Arctic have used packed snow to build shelters called igloos.

An Iowa newspaper was the first use the word "blizzard" on April 23, 1870.

At 89.3 inches (227 cm), Vermont has the highest statewide average annual snowfall.

Minneapolis–St. Paul International Airport uses heated pools of water to melt snow.

Ottawa, Canada, is the snowiest national capital. It averages 93 inches (236 cm) of snow annually.

Fifteen inches (38.1 cm) of snow equals about 1 inch (2.5 cm) of rain.

The snowiest village

in the U.S. is Alta, Utah.

It averages 583 inches (1,481 cm) per year.

FEBRUARY 3–8, 1972

Xtreme Snowstorm #1

The 1972 Iran Blizzard In February 1972, a six-day blizzard hit Iran. It ended a four-year drought, but snow fell 10 to 26 feet (3-7.9 m) deep. It buried entire villages. The temperature dropped to -13 °F (-25 °C). Pipes froze. People lost heat. They went days without food, water, or medical aid. In some remote villages, all of the residents died. The storm killed about 4,000 people. It is the deadliest blizzard in recorded history.

GLOSSARY

blizzards – storms that last at least 3 hours with winds of 35 miles (56.3 km) per hour or greater and reduced visibility

cannibalism – the act of eating the flesh of the same species

equator – the imaginary line around the center of the globe, halfway between the North and South poles

evaporates – changes from a liquid to a gas

RESOURCES

Farndon, John. *Extreme Weather*. New York: Dorling Kindersley, 2007.

Grabianoski, Ed. How Stuff Works: Science. "10 Biggest Snowstorms of All Time." http://science.howstuffworks.com /nature/climate-weather/storms/10-biggest-snowstorms.htm.

Laskin, David. *The Children's Blizzard*. New York: HarperCollins, 2004.

U.S. Environmental Protection Agency. "Climate Change Indicators: Snow and Ice." http://www3.epa.gov/climatechange /science/indicators/snow-ice/.

INDEX

benefits 20, 21

blizzards 8, 16, 21, 26, 28, 31

dangers 8, 11, 16, 21, 26, 28, 31

formation conditions 5, 12, 15, 18, 19

glaciers 25

human interaction with snow 5, 8, 20, 28

infamous snowstorms 10, 16, 21, 22, 26, 31

mountains 8, 10, 19, 21, 28

snow removal 20, 21, 28

snowfall occurrences 6, 7, 18, 19, 22, 28, 31

snowfall totals 6, 7, 19, 22, 24, 28, 29, 31

snowflake features 4, 8, 9, 12, 15, 28

Snow appears white, but it is in fact clear.